Lots of Frogs

By Sally Cowan

There are lots of frogs.

Frogs look wet, and some frogs have dots and blobs.

Some frogs have frills!

This frog has a frill
on its back leg.

frill

Frogs have homes in bogs.

Bogs have wet rocks
and logs.

Frogs can get lots of fresh food in bogs.

Frogs are quick!

They can get ants and bugs.

They get moths, too.

Zap!

They lick them up!

Frogs have long back legs.

They can do big hops
off the rocks.

Frogs can have lots and lots of eggs.

Some frogs have eggs in froth.

eggs in froth

Frogs nap in the day.

But when the sun sets,
the frogs sing!

It's fun to look at frogs!

This frog is singing.

CHECKING FOR MEANING

1.   Where do frogs live? *(Literal)*

2.   What do frogs find to eat in the bogs? *(Literal)*

3.   Why do you think some frogs put their eggs in froth? *(Inferential)*

EXTENDING VOCABULARY

frill	What is a *frill*? Other than on a frog, where else would you find a frill?
fresh	What is *fresh* food? How is it different to food that is not fresh?
froth	What is another word for *froth* in this book? What is something a frog eats that rhymes with *froth*?

MOVING BEYOND THE TEXT

1. What colours can frogs be?

2. Have you seen a frog in your garden or in a pond? What colour was it? What food would it eat?

3. Discuss the simple life cycle of a frog.

4. What sounds do frogs make? Do they sing?

SPEED SOUNDS

bl	gl	cr	fr	st

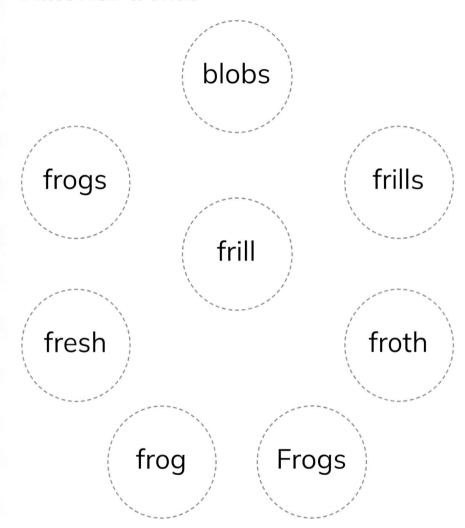

blobs

frogs

frills

frill

fresh

froth

frog

Frogs